Choose Life! The Two Ways

CHOOSE
LIFE
THE TWO WAYS

by
FRANCES
HOGAN

Collins
FLAME

William Collins Sons & Co. Ltd

London • Glasgow • Sydney • Auckland

Toronto • Johannesburg

First published in Great Britain in 1990 by Flame

Flame is an imprint of
Collins Religious Division,
part of the Collins Publishing Group
8 Grafton Street, London W1X 3LA

Printed and bound in Great Britain by
Courier International Ltd, Tiptree, Essex

Choose Life! The Two Ways

DEUTERONOMY 30:16–20

"Look, today I am offering you life and prosperity, death and disaster. If you obey the commandments of the Lord your God, which I am laying down for you today, if you love the Lord your God and follow his ways . . . you will live and grow numerous, and the Lord your God will bless you in the country which you are about to enter and make your own. But if your heart turns away, if you refuse to listen, if you let yourself be drawn into worshipping other gods and serving them, I tell you today, you will most certainly perish. . . . Today I call heaven and earth to witness against you: I am offering you life or death, blessing or curse. Choose life, then, so that you and your descendants may live in the love of the Lord your God, obeying his voice, holding fast to him; for in this your life consists, and on this depends the length of time that you stay in the country. . . ."

This was the advice given by Moses to the Chosen People prior to their entry into the Promised Land. Basically he told them that there were two ways to live one's life, namely in conformity to God's plan for the human race, or to do one's own thing. Or to put it simply, the choice was between God's will and self-will, with long-lasting consequences to going either way. In presenting this choice to his people Moses understood with regard to human beings what we in the twentieth century understand of machines, namely that the manufacturer knows the machine he made better than anyone else! He knows how it works: he knows what

5

fouls it up, and he knows what to do when it breaks down, hence he supplies a manufacturer's handbook with the relevant instructions. The new buyer would be foolish indeed not to read this manual, for the long life of the machine is at stake.

Moses was not the first teacher to present THE TWO WAYS to the human race. The Book of Genesis tells us that those who guided God's people way back in the dim and distant past presented the same choice to their audiences when they spoke of the tree of life and the tree of the knowledge of good and evil (Gen. 2.17). The tree of life represented God's way, the way of wisdom, while the other one represented life lived according to one's own whims and desires. There are no marks for knowing the dreadful result of the choice of the tree of the knowledge of good and evil in Eden. Have we not inherited it? Who taught us as children to stamp our feet and insist on our own way? Who taught us to insist on learning by experience when it would be much easier to learn from others? Why do we say that only those things learned by experience actually stay with us? Oh yes, there is a decision deep within the heart of the human race to choose OUR OWN WAY, to do what we want regardless of consequences. That choice is self-will, with all its consequent evils of manipulating and controlling others, of using and abusing them in order to make life comfortable for ourselves.

This choice puts self in the centre of our lives, while pushing others and God to the periphery. Love is the opposite of this, as we discover when we "fall in love", because it puts the other person in the centre and pushes the self to one side. Notice how happy people are when they fall in love! They are constantly thinking of the beloved, wanting to make all kinds of sacrifices for them to make them happy, for ever contacting them to see how they are, and wanting to be with the beloved. So we become happy (as experience shows us!) when we lay aside self and selfishness for the sake of a greater good, in order to become a source of life and joy to others.

SELF-WILL/SELF-SERVICE

Before we consider the tree of life let us look at the service of self, so that our choices become clearer and simpler. There is nothing more universal than self-will. It is found in the youngest infant and the oldest grandparent. It is one of those things that must be disciplined or it becomes a tyrant which destroys all before it. We either conquer self-will or it conquers us. There is no halfway position. It is the will to rule, demanding power and control as its right. This is evidenced even in babies. How quickly they become tyrants when their needs are allowed to dominate a household! Whereas the disciplined child remains a lovely child, one who is easy to love, and therefore draws love to itself. The tyrant, on the other hand, draws rejection and punishment upon itself instead. Selfishness and self-will make a person unloving and unlovable, turned in on themselves, locked into a tiny world of "me" and "my" to the exclusion of all else.

Selfishness is easy to recognize in the whims of an innocent child, but can we recognize the same principle in the political tyrant? In terrorist gangs, and all forms of organized crime? Can we see it in the autocratic and self-opinionated behaviour of parents who dominate a home with their whims and demands to the exclusion of the needs of other members? Do we recognize it in the self-appointed leader of a prayer group, or any other parish group who is there for their own needs rather than for service? Self-will, selfishness, and self-indulgence come in many forms, some of which look religious, but selfishness is definitely not religious! It is very worldly and belongs to the realm of the flesh, of ungraced human nature, in need of redemption.

THE STORY OF SAUL

The Old Testament supplies us with examples of both good and evil so that we will learn from them—and hopefully not repeat the bad examples! As Paul told Timothy in 2 Timothy 3:16 "All scripture is inspired by God and useful for refuting error, for guiding people's lives and teaching them to be upright". So let us learn from the bad example of King Saul. His story is told in the First Book of Samuel beginning at chapter 8 where the people of Israel demand a king for the first time in their history. Samuel, the prophet, warned them not to choose a king and spelled out the consequences for them, but they would not listen, for they wanted to be like all other nations, and they had kings.

Saul was chosen by lot and consecrated king by Samuel, who prophesied over him that he would experience a great change in his life when the Holy Spirit came upon him that very day, making him God's officially anointed servant, and shepherd of His people Israel; therefore responsible for the keeping of the covenant Israel had made with God (I Sam. 9–10). Initially Saul was humble and small in his own eyes. When the people went to look for him to crown him king he hid among the baggage (I Sam. 10.23). He was also kind and compassionate in his first victory over his enemies (I Sam. 11.25). Nevertheless Saul had one fatal flaw: it was self-will. As a private citizen it would have affected himself and his immediate family, but now as head of state it was to take on national importance, for in those days what the king did the people did. He was not only the political and military leader but the model for the people also.

If the king did not choose to do God's will there would be far-reaching consequences, both for himself and for the nation. Samuel resigned to give Saul full responsibility for the nation (I Sam. 12), but before handing over, Samuel reminded both king and people of Moses' instruction: " . . . the Lord your God himself is your King, (but) here is the king you have chosen; the Lord has set a king over you. If you reverence and serve the Lord and obey his voice and do not rebel against his order, and if both you and the king who rules over you follow the Lord your God, all will be well. But if you do not obey the voice of the Lord your God, if you rebel against his order, his hand will be against you and against your king."

With this clear reminder that both national and family peace depended on obedience to the will of God, Samuel left the scene thinking his job was done, but not so. Power went quickly to Saul's head, and the ugly face of self-will began to show itself. Samuel had to confront him several times on the importance of obedience to God's will. To act otherwise was to act like a fool (I Sam. 13:13).

This wrung out of Samuel one of the greatest statements in the Bible regarding obedience to God. It is in I Sam. 15.23: "Is the pleasure of the Lord in holocausts and sacrifices or in obedience to the voice of the Lord? Yes, obedience is better than sacrifice, submissiveness better than the fat of rams. Rebellion is a sin of sorcery, presumption a crime of teraphim." Saul was deceiving himself if he thought that offering animals to God in sacrifice was "good religion" when he refused to carry out God's explicit orders. True worship is doing God's Will. God is not willing to be fobbed off with ritual when He demands obedience. Psalm 50 gives very clear warning on this point. In verses 7–13 God says that He wants no more sacrifices, for He owns all the animals they are killing. He wants obedience to the covenant they made with Him! It is so easy for us to think that we are worshipping God when we attend religious services, but the essence of worship is to sacrifice our own will to God. In the second half of the psalm God demands obedience to the commandments as the sign of real religion.

> "Let thanksgiving be your sacrifice to God,
> fulfill the vows you make to the Most High;
> Then if you call to me in time of trouble
> I will rescue you and you will honour me"
>
> (v.14).

Saul's problem was that he would do God's will if it suited him, otherwise no. When he thought that God's command – given either through the covenant or through the prophet – was unreasonable he did not obey. He did what he thought best in the circumstances. Scripture is very clear on one thing, that God cannot use a person who does their own thing. He needs servants who do His will, for only then can His kingdom come. Hence Saul was rejected as king and the Lord sent Samuel the prophet to seek a man after God's own heart, namely an obedient servant (I Sam.

13:14). God instructed Samuel not to be impressed by external appearances, for it was the condition of the heart that was the important thing (I Sam. 16:7).

Very soon the story reveals the condition of Saul's heart. Something which was known only to God initially, was eventually revealed to all as the fruits of his life began to show. Jesus told us in Matthew 7.15–20 that a sound tree cannot bear bad fruit, nor a rotten tree good fruit. It is what comes out of the life eventually that reveals what was there all the time. What eventually emerged from Saul's life was bad indeed. I Samuel 16:14 states that – eventually – "the spirit of the Lord had left Saul and an evil spirit from the Lord filled him with terror". Since the Israelites believed that God was the source of everything, God had permitted this evil presence to take up residence in Saul's life. The entrance of the evil spirit had to be through sin, and self-will is the basic sin. Saul's disobedience opened the way to evil for him, and for the nation which suffered under his erratic rule.

Now that Saul had lost the presence of the Lord, he also lost the divine protection that went with it, leaving him helpless before his enemies who defied and threatened him (I Sam. 17). It should have been a good lesson for him to see the innocent and obedient servant of the Lord, David, conquer the enemy without any difficulty because the Lord was on his side. Yet, instead of emulating the boy, Saul became envious and jealous of him, to such an extent that he tried to murder him (I Sam. 18:9–10). When he could not succeed in killing David himself Saul tried to kill him in battle (I Sam. 18:25), but he failed in this plan also because David was so successful in war that all Israel revered him. Saul then became his implacable enemy, so that David was forced to become a fugitive for years, deprived of all justice and normal life.

During this period David was constantly hunted down by Saul who gave him no respite. Nevertheless David twice showed mercy to his enemy in dramatic ways when Saul fell into his grasp (I Sam. 24, 26). Saul was deeply moved on each occasion by this forgiveness, but he did not repent. He did not change his ways, and continued to hunt David as if nothing had happened. It seemed at this stage that nothing could get through to Saul's hardened heart. Instead of caring for his kingdom he gave his time and attention mainly to hunting David. He was falling deeper and deeper into iniquity.

After Samuel died, Saul, who was no longer in contact with the Lord in prayer, turned to witchcraft to find help, but found despair instead, and the gruesome message of his own death the following day (I Sam. 28). The end of this saga came as Saul engaged the Philistines in battle even though he had been warned that it would only bring disaster to himself, his family, and his army. But a self-willed person will not listen to others, so when he was wounded in battle he committed suicide (I Sam. 31). A sad end to a privileged life. It was all so unnecessary too, for this strong will of his could have been a great asset if it had been disciplined and harnessed for good. What we see instead is that something left untamed and untouched by grace will take over and ruin our lives as well as the lives of others. Self-will is one power that definitely must be put under the control of grace or we will be controlled by it. Learn from the tragedy of Saul.

DOWN THE SLIPPERY SLOPE

Jesus told a wonderful parable concerning a traveller on the read from Jerusalem to Jericho near the Dead

Sea (Luke 10:29–37). Jerusalem is approximately 2,500 feet above sea level and Jericho is about 1,300 feet below sea level. To travel to Jericho along that road meant going downhill all the way. Now, in Luke's gospel, Jerusalem is the centre of everything. It is the city of destiny and the home of the House of God. The whole gospel is a journey to Jerusalem, even for Jesus, who will find his destiny there like all the prophets before him. So the traveller in the story is on the right road but in the wrong direction. Jericho represents the worldly city, the sin-city. Hot as hell in the summer, it is the winter resort for the idle rich.

The traveller in the story represents everyone on the road to life. We are pilgrims on our way to the heavenly city, and the destiny that God has planned for us in His loving mercy. It is essential that we not only find the right road, but also the right direction. It is no laughing matter to find oneself on the slippery slope in life, for it leads to destruction. One should never travel alone either as the journey is too dangerous. The story tells us that this poor traveller was set upon by robbers who took everything he had, beat him up and left him lying there half dead. He would surely have died had not the providence of God sent him some neighbours to rescue him.

Some of those who met him were no use as helpers. They were too taken up with themselves and their own little world to care about anyone else. They were self-centred even in their religion, which of course makes a mockery of religion, for true religion is concerned with God's kingdom and the service of others. If we truly loved God we would love our neighbour also, as one is the measure of the other. St John says that it is not possible to love God whom you do not see if you do not love the neighbour whom you do see (I John 4.20).

The poor victim dying on the road would be in a sorry state if a real neighbour did not come along, one whose love is other-centred, spontaneous, kind, personal and effective! The dying man is a personification of the teaching of St Paul that the wages of sin is death (Rom. 6:23), and the Good Samaritan is a personification of the work of Jesus, our Saviour, and of all those who work in His name, who have the privilege of acting on the Lord's behalf to bring healing and redemption to sinners. To heal them and leave them on the road where we found them is certainly no solution, for that is where tragedy struck. They cannot be left where they were. They must be healed, and helped to get back on their feet, given a place in the Lord's house (the inn) and set on the right road, in the right direction.

WHAT IS THE SLIPPERY SLOPE?

The two ways were seen in that parable, for one road led to Jerusalem and all that God intended for us while the other led to worldliness, sin, destruction and finally death. How does one get on to the wrong way? How does it start? Can we stop it? Can we turn back? Can we recognize what is happening to us? We will see! Psalm I also speaks of the two ways, but from a different angle to Moses. The psalmist looks at the fruits of a person's life and then tells you who you are speaking to! This enables us to discern the problem in others, and then, hopefully to take a good look at ourselves!

How blessed is anyone who rejects the advice of
   the wicked
and does not take a stand in the path that sinners
   tread,

14

nor a seat in company with cynics,
but who delights in the law of the Lord
and murmurs his law day and night.

Such a one is like a tree planted near streams.
it bears fruit in season
and its leaves never wither,
and every project succeeds.
How different the wicked, how different!

Just like chaff blown around by the wind
the wicked will not stand firm at Judgement
nor sinners in the gathering of the upright,
but the path of the wicked is doomed.

The psalmist divides human beings into two categories, the upright and the wicked. He describes the two different ways of life led by them, and the end product of their existence, leaving you, the reader, to judge for yourself which is the correct one to choose. The upright and the wicked are on two different paths in life. The upright are not "goody-goody" people. They are not good all the time. They are just people who are on the right road, in the right direction. They are in contact with God in prayer where they can get the help and grace needed for life's decisions. Nor are the wicked bad all the time. King Saul had many good traits. Judas, the traitor, had good traits too, while Peter had some traits that needed to be changed. Yet Judas and Peter were on two different paths, indicated by the simple fact that Peter was open to learn and to change, and he received correction from Jesus, whereas Judas was closed, refused to learn or change, and ended by bringing death to both Jesus and himself.

So the wicked are not bad all the time and the upright are not good all the time. The thing that matters is what direction your life is taking right now. Where is it going? Are you headed for a greater and greater conformity to God's will, or are you hardening into self-will? There lies the answer, for this is the basic decision before each one of us. In the final analysis we either serve God or ourselves. While this decision is taken in the privacy of our own hearts, the fruits of it are obvious to everyone, as Psalm I tells us. (Psalm 2 says that nations also take the decision for or against God's way).

The psalmist says that anyone walking God's way will not be found taking advice from the wicked, because that advice would concern their own way of life, which leads to disaster. The upright cannot go there for help. They must seek it from those who are on the right way. Neither can they seek fellowship from the wicked, for their evil influence would harm them, nor will they be found with the cynics and unbelievers. So we are told to look at the company one keeps to find the influences on a person's life, for we humans are very affected by each other's thinking. And thinking always leads to action sooner or later.

The upright will be found leading a prayer life, seeking wisdom from the holy scriptures, and finding fellowship with others on that road. Since they delight in God's will they grow strong spiritually and their lives mature into mellow fruitfulness in every way, just like the great cedars of Lebanon. Since their lives are founded on the rock of truth and salvation they can survive the storms of life and face the Day of Judgment without fear.

The fate of the wicked is very different from this. Having lived their lives on the sand of their own will, and indulged all their passions as they pleased, they become weaker. There is no substance to their lives. There is nothing in them that can outlast life. Indeed their self-indulgence can be the cause of their illnesses, of both body and soul. They are the source of their own misery. Sooner or later they face an old age of fear and loneliness, with the spectre of a wasted life to haunt their final hours. The Day of Judgment is not a subject that can be brought up in their presence, for they fear death more than anything else, while their wise neighbours face death and beyond with peace of mind. Whatever lies beyond death, they are sure that they have led the best life they could here and they leave with no regrets.

Let us express the teaching of this psalm in Jesus' own words in Matthew 7.21–27. In this text Jesus does not accept the "Lord, Lord" approach to religion, when the bottom line is that we must do the will of the Father. He says that prayers that do not include commitment to God's will are useless and won't be heard. It is religion on the rocks in contrast to a proper spiritual life founded on commitment to God's will: "Therefore, everyone who listens to these words of mine *and acts on them* will be like a sensible man who built his house on rock. Rain came down, floods rose, gales blew and hurled themselves against that house, and it did not fall: it was founded on rock. But everyone who listens to these words of mine *and does not act on them* will be like a stupid man who built his house on sand. Rain came down, floods rose, gales blew and struck that house, and it fell; and what a fall it had!"

SLAVERY TO SELF

"In all truth I tell you, everyone who commits sin is a slave" (John 8.34). These stark words of Jesus put the whole matter in a nutshell. If we choose our own will we soon learn that it is a corrupted will, born into a sinful and sinning world. We learn sooner or later that our choices are not always good, even for ourselves. The will in the service of the self soon becomes a slave to sin. Sin blinds the heart to good, and we are on the slippery slope in real earnest.

Paul's description of the world in his own day reads like tomorrow's newspaper to us. He describes society in the grip of sin and its consequent misery. He describes a world rejecting God, and rejecting good, a society given to injustice and violence; a people who indulge every passion, no longer satisfied with normal sexual relationships but turning to homosexuality: "And so now they are steeped in all sorts of injustice, rottenness, greed and malice; full of envy, murder, wrangling, treachery and spite, libellers, slanderers, enemies of God, rude, arrogant, and boastful, enterprising in evil, rebellious to parents, without brains, honour, love or pity. They are well aware of God's ordinance that those who behave like this deserve to die – yet they not only do it, but even applaud others who do the same" (Rom. 1.18–32). This is slavery, even if the country we live in enjoys political freedom. Can the acceptance of hedonism today be called "freedom"? Look at its consequences in the breakdown of family life and the misery of millions of children, and the answer is clear. It is death not life.

With the world given over to corruption where are the religious people? Are they not the salt of the earth preserving and purifying the dough? Surely if the religious people were worth their weight in salt the world would not get into such a mess. Paul says that the religious people are infected by the same disease! The fact that *you know what is right* is no guarantee that you can *do what is right*. To do what is right we need the help of God and grace (Rom. 2). Paul's judgment is that all have sinned. Quoting several of the psalms Paul says that not one of us is upright, not a single one (Rom. 3.9–20). We are all in need of the liberation of mind and heart that Jesus came to bring us.

THE END OF THE ROAD

Where does the slippery slope lead to? We know that the parable said it led to Jericho, but what is that in everyday life? What does it represent at the end of life? Is there a sequel to the story, or does it finish with Jericho? Let us look briefly at Psalm 37 which treats of the fate of the good and the wicked. The psalmist is quite clear that the two ways have very different ends, so it is wise to consider them. In dealing with the wicked the psalmist is dealing with those who are given over to worldliness, unbelief, selfishness and immorality in a gross way. Self is at the centre of their world and all others, including God, are pushed aside, but we are not dealing with criminals. We are dealing with people whom the world applauds, and honours: as Psalm 49.19 says rightly that "people praise you for looking after yourself".

First, the good are told not to envy the wicked because they will wither as quickly as the grass in the field (vv. 1–2). Life is short, and the end of that life determines the eternal destiny of the person. Shakespeare expressed the same thought when he said that "we strut and fret our hour upon the stage and then are heard no more". The good are advised to trust their fate into the Lord's hands, and make Him their only joy, for then He will give them their hearts' desires (vv. 3–4). God will act on behalf of the good, but they must wait patiently for Him, and live a life of virtue (vv. 5–7). They should not worry about the wicked making their fortunes at the expense of the poor, nor indulge in anger, for anything created out of evil will have an evil end (v. 7–10). That "evil end" may not be apparent to us, but God has everything under control. He sees everything, including the killing of innocent victims for whatever reason, whether that death is physical, mental or spiritual.

However the peace that the good possess is worth more than all the power and wealth of the wicked put together. The Lord takes care of their lives and sees to their needs in times of trouble (vv. 11–19), but "The wicked, enemies of the Lord, will be destroyed, they will vanish like the green of the pasture, they will vanish in smoke" (v. 20). Meanwhile the Lord guides the steps of the good. Even if they fall into sin it won't be fatal, for God is there to help them get up and go on. He teaches them to be generous with their material goods and to be compassionate to those who suffer. Because of this their descendants will have the blessing of God, as good deeds live on, but the descendants of the wicked have the shade of evil to live with (vv. 21–26). The good are cautioned: "Never yield to evil, practise good and you will have an everlasting home, for the Lord loves what is right, and never deserts the devout" (vv. 27–28).

The good put their hope in God and His goodness,

and become wise through keeping the Commandments, and studying God's Word. They receive salvation from the Lord, who delights to help them: "The Lord helps them and rescues them, he saves them because they take shelter in him." And this salvation is not just for now but for all eternity. They find their true home with the Lord. Their peace and joy will last for ever. Meanwhile the wicked spy on them and persecute them, but it recoils on their own heads: "I have seen the wicked in his triumph towering like the cedar of Lebanon, but when next I passed, he was not there, I looked for him and he was nowhere to be found" (vv. 30–40). To be lost eternally is the ultimate tragedy, too unspeakable to mention. What is the point in all the political or social power if it costs one's eternal life? Let us listen to the words of Jesus: "What gain, then, is it for anyone to win the world and forfeit his life?" (Mark 8.36). What is the point in being an emperor in Hell? Would it not be better to be a floor-sweeper in Heaven, where one is surrounded by love, joy and peace?

Psalm 49 speaks eloquently about the futility of riches, when that is *all* one has. Wealth is dangerous because of what it does to us. Human beings seem not to be able to handle wealth for it appears to insulate us from reality, and from the spiritual world, and we quickly come to the point where we think that everything can be bought – even salvation. Many give up the notion of God altogether as soon as they become rich. In other words they exchange everything for nothing.

The author of this psalm tells us that he has wisdom to share both from his observations on life, and from his own experience. We will do well to take heed (vv. 1–6). The first thing to note is that all human beings desperately need salvation, and *that* cannot be bought with money, otherwise the rich would all be saved and the poor lost for ever. "But no one can ever redeem himself or pay his own ransom to God, the price for himself is too high; it can never be that he will live on for ever and avoid the sight of the abyss" (vv. 7–9).

The second observation is that both rich and poor die, the wise and foolish also die: the good and the wicked die. When then? Well, the rich have to leave their fortunes to others, and they end up, like the poor, in a grave 6 feet by 3 feet. Who is to know which corpse is the more important when they are both actively decaying? When they are both forgotten so quickly? It makes no difference *now* that one of them owned estates during his lifetime, and had servants running after him. What did either of them have that could outlast life? "For ever no home but their tombs, their dwelling place age after age, though they gave their name to whole territories" (vv. 10–11).

Of what value is the show they made now? What do they think now of their behaviour towards the poor? Their self-importance means nothing here in a grave six feet by three feet. They are just the same as all other corpses, even if they did have a lavish funeral. Death is death, and decomposure is decay no matter who you are. It is the ultimate leveller of the human race. "They are penned in Sheol (the place of the dead) like sheep, Death will lead them to pasture, and those who are honest will rule over them. In the morning all trace of them will be gone, Sheol will be their home. But my soul God will ransom from the clutches of Sheol, and will snatch me up" (vv. 14–15).

Here we are told that the ultimate destiny of the good and the wicked are different. Death is personified to let us see that the wicked do not see heaven (God's home), that there is retribution beyond the grave where there is no court of appeal, and no one to bribe with money. It is ultimate justice, something everyone fears. Therefore the psalmist warns us not to be overawed when people grow rich, for the responsibility of riches is great, and so many people let wealth go to their heads and forfeit their true life and their true destiny as a result.

Jesus told a parable about this in Luke 16.19–31. Dives was the rich man and Lazarus the poor, sick one. Dives pampered himself while neglecting his responsibility to the poor man. He lived only for himself, but not for his *real life*. Self-indulgence is not real living, for it is self-destructive. The fate of both men is clearly shown. Lazarus escaped Sheol and was now in Abraham's bosom, while Dives lies in Hell. If Dives had used his wealth properly and taken care of Lazarus, then the poor man would have praised him to God, and Dives would have had an intercessor where it mattered most. Lazarus would have pleaded his cause. Do we realize how badly we need those we help? Do we realize how much we need the blessing of the poor?

The Book of Proverbs says (Prov. 21.23) "He who shuts his ear to the poor man's cry shall himself plead and not be heard". This is what happened to Dives, so we can see why Psalm 49 repeatedly says that we forfeit intelligence or common sense when we grow rich. The rich need the poor more than the poor need them. The poor only need material help, but the wealthy need intercessors before God to plead for their salvation. This does not mean, of course, that there are no good people among the rich, but as a general principle it speaks of the deadening effect that wealth has on people who are tempted to live for this world only.

Let us leave the last word to Jesus: "How hard it is for those who have riches to make their way into the kingdom of God! Yes, it is easier for a camel to pass through the eye of a needle than for someone rich to enter the kingdom of God". Those who were listening said, "In that case, who can be saved?" He replied, "Things that are impossible by human resources, are possible with God" (Luke 18.24–27).

CAN RELIGIOUS PEOPLE LOSE THEIR WAY?

Do the wicked only include the ungodly, the immoral, the unbelievers, the criminal? Is it possible for those who *look good* not to be good? Is it possible to stray from the right path and thus find oneself on the right road but in the wrong direction? You better believe it! It is always possible for us to turn aside from the right path, so constant vigilance is necessary. Jesus warned us repeatedly concerning this. The journey we have undertaken is a dangerous one, fraught with difficulties. Some of these originate with ourselves, some from fellow travellers, and some from the evil one himself. The world also causes problems by laughing at our simplicity to believe at all, maybe even by persecution.

Listen to Jesus: "Watch yourselves, or your hearts will be coarsened by debauchery and drunkenness and the cares of life, and that day (death, or the Day of Judgment) will come upon you unexpectedly . . . Stay awake, praying at all times for the strength to survive . . . and to hold your ground before the Son of Man" (Luke 21.34–36). It is possible for someone who was open once to close up and no longer listen to truth, or to the Lord. The people who most opposed Jesus during his lifetime were not the sinners in dire need of redemption, but the religious people who should have known better. Jesus found them closed to the gospel. They had become slaves to the Law, even though the Law in its own right was a good thing and had originated with God. But the Law was meant to educate in truth not enslave them in rules and legalities (see Rom. 7.1–13).

The Law was difficult to obey in all its prescriptions as the Apostles later admitted (Acts 15.10), so when the Pharisees made great sacrifices to keep the Law, they fell into the problem of self-righteousness. They were convinced that they were saved by keeping even the most minute prescriptions of the Law, yet they were not open to receive the forgiveness of Jesus, because that entailed admitting one had sinned! The self-righteous do not see themselves as sinners.

This is portrayed in the parable of the Pharisee and the Tax Collector in Luke 18.9–14, where the Pharisee tells God how good he is in keeping the Law, and how religious he is in fasting and praying. And the point is that *he was good* if we compare him with ungodly sinners! But would you like to be God in that monologue? This man needed no Saviour. He was praising himself, not God. When he compared himself with the rest of his adulterous generation he did quite well. He scored 10/10. Not bad for a human being who is supposed to be weak when tempted! No one could bring up the subject of forgiveness here. It was not needed.

The self-righteous have an "I" problem that must be dealt with, for they become bloated with pride in their own achievements. While they would never descend to the filthy sins of the worldly, they cannot see that their self-centred existence is no different. It is just as worldly, but more dangerous because their sins cannot be seen so easily. Pride and arrogance are difficult to detect in oneself, just as difficult as self-righteousness. Just as difficult as being closed to the grace of God. Jesus warned the Pharisees of his own day that they were in grave danger of being left outside of the kingdom of God, not for want of an invitation, or a Saviour, but because they were closed to both. This is the message of the parable of the great supper in Luke 14.15–24.

Just before the Passion, as many sinners had joined Jesus and begun the great journey of salvation, while they were all, literally, on their way to Jerusalem, Jesus gave a final warning to the religious leaders that they were in danger of finding themselves locked out of the heavenly banquet. Not only that but they would see their places taken by the very sinners that they despised!

"Once the master of the house (Jesus) has got up (risen from the dead) and locked the door (on Israel's Day of Salvation), you may find yourself standing outside knocking on the door, saying, 'Lord, open to us', but he will answer, 'I do not know where you come from' (because only those redeemed by Jesus are within). Then you will start saying, 'We once ate and drank in your company; you taught in our streets' (thinking they can 'pull strings' from relationship, nationality or privilege) but he will reply, 'I do not know where you come from; *away from me, all evil doers!*' (those who do their own will, and refuse to open to God and salvation). Then there will be weeping and grinding of teeth (a description of Hell), when you see Abraham, Isaac and Jacob and all the prophets in the kingdom of God, *and yourselves thrown out.* And people from east and west, from north and south, will come and sit down at the feast in the kingdom of God. (Even Gentiles from all over the world will be there.) "Look, there are those now last (sinners and Gentiles) who will be first, and those now first (Jews and religious leaders) who will be last" (where it matters most!). It's the end of the road that matters. Where are you headed?

THE ROAD TO JERUSALEM

"Who shall climb the mountain of the Lord? Who shall stand in His Holy Place? (Ps. 14). How do we find our way to the tree of life? In Luke 4.18 Jesus declared that he came to set the captives free, to give new sight to the blind, and to free all those who are oppressed. Jesus has the answer. By now we realize that true freedom is *internal*, as bondage is also. We in the so-called free world find that while we are politically free many are enslaved to capitalism, materialism and godlessness. The real god that we pay homage to is money or Mammon, and the second one is self. This is interior slavery or bondage of a type that is difficult to eradicate. What we need more than anything else is internal freedom or freedom of the heart, and this is precisely what Jesus offers.

One of the basic gifts that God had endowed us with is free will, and He has always held us responsible for our free choices. Freedom and responsibility go together. Responsibility is the burden of freedom. In Genesis 3, God held both Adam and Eve responsible for the choices they made; even though Adam appeared more passive than Eve, he was held responsible for his passive choice, and dealt with accordingly.

In Genesis 4, God held Cain responsible for his

choices too. He expected him to take authority over himself and resist the urge to kill his brother, thus enslaving himself. When Cain refused to control his desires God punished him as a responsible person. He did not hold him temporarily insane as many courts do today. God was willing to help Cain deal with the problem, but Cain *would not listen*, and ended up doing his own thing. Cain refused the help of God, as so many people do today who refuse to listen to God speak to them in the holy scriptures, through the teaching of the Church, and in personal prayer. This refusal is a decision for which we must take the consequences as Cain did.

Our future is not a mystery, for it is forged out of the daily choices that we make on so many issues. Many of these choices appear trivial at the time, and it may seem difficult to believe that they could have far reaching consequences. Yet we know that a woollen cardigan is made up of many individual stitches, that cloth is woven from many very fine threads, just as relationships are forged from smiles or grimaces and many tiny decisions concerning what appear to be small matters. If you want to know which direction your path is taking, whether you are headed towards Jerusalem or not, then sit down and examine your conduct. Look at your decisions and you will see clearly enough, for we are daily choosing our destiny. It is the choices we make today that determine our tomorrows!

What is needed is a combination of grace freely given by the Lord and our full, free cooperation with it to accomplish our salvation. This is seen in the dramatic conversion of Saul to become the great missionary Paul (see Acts 22.6–21). How this combination works is a mystery, for only God knows how to touch our hearts with effective grace without interfering with our free choice (see Hos. 2.16–22). As Paul was able to say later in life: "What I am now, I am through the grace of God, and the grace which was given to me has not been wasted" (I Cor. 15.10).

INVITATION TO FREEDOM

Jesus gave the invitation to freedom in Matthew 11.28–30: "Come to me, all you who labour and are over-burdened, and I will give you rest. Shoulder my yoke and learn from me, for I am gentle and humble of heart, *and you will find rest for your souls.* Yes, my yoke is easy and my burden light." This is a passionate plea from Christ to all of us to come over to His side, to join Him, if we want to know freedom, peace and happiness. He alone can show us the way back to the Father, for he himself IS THE WAY, THE TRUTH AND THE LIFE (John 14.6). When Jesus looked at the people of his own day He saw them weighed down by so many burdens, political and social, but most of all the burden of sin. They were in bondage to so many things, yet He offered only one solution: "Come to Me"! It seems too simple for so many complex issues.

In this invitation he offered them relief, healing and fulfilment. Under the heading of relief he offered the forgiveness of sin, thus lifting the weight of guilt which can be so heavy as to grind us to a halt in life. Through his death and resurrection he broke the chains of sin, death and hell which held the human race bound for so long. He also lifts the burden of anxiety, which leaves us free to seek God again (see Matt. 6.25–34). He gave back to life a sense of purpose, thus lifting the dead weight of meaninglessness off our existence, so that we can exclaim with the psalmist, "You have turned my mourning into dancing, you have stripped off my sackcloth and clothed me with joy. So my heart will sing to you unceasingly. Oh Lord my God I will praise you forever" (Ps. 30.11–12).

But that is not all. He has taken away the burden of a meaningless death, making it into a gateway into glory. And he has taken away the threat of Hell for those who seek the Lord and follow his ways. Fear of Hell keeps many people away from the Church: ironically, they just cannot face such a possibility. Yet they may not be willing to listen as we explain how they can pass from death to life in the here and now, and escape Hell altogether in the next life.

Those who do not seek the Lord need to receive the sound warning I read in a small English village some years ago. There was a preservation order on the whole village so a house that was blocking the traffic could not be demolished. Instead the yellow box sign was put on the road around the house to keep the traffic moving freely. A huge notice concerning this "yellow box" was put on the gable end of the house where all motorists could read it on approach. It read: "Don't enter the box unless your exit is clear". Whoever put the notice there must not have checked to see that the house was now being used as a funeral parlour, with a coffin in the window! All motorists approaching the house saw the COFFIN and read: "Don't enter the box unless your exit is clear"! I couldn't agree more! It is very dangerous to crashland into eternity.

Jesus not only forgives, but also heals the scars left from our sinfulness. He also heals the wounds and scars left from the sinfulness of others we live and work with. His powerful grace goes to the very core of our being with inner healing of our emotions, the healing of mind, heart and body. It is complete redemption that

31

he offers, not just "a religion" – whatever that is! With forgiveness and healing he also offers us a relationship of love and friendship with himself, one that begins now but lasts into eternity. " . . . the love of God has been poured into our hearts by the Holy Spirit which has been given to us" (Rom. 5.5).

This relationship is what gives us a sense of security both for time and eternity, not just a good feeling, but the realization that we have found what we were made for, that we are on the road to Life. This increases our sense of self-worth, for we are loved by the greatest love in the universe. It also gives a sense of destiny, and makes even very ordinary people "a very important somebody" in the eyes of God. Married couples become "very important somebodies" to each other, and to their children. Love does that sort of thing. When we join ourselves to the Lord, then we become important to Him, to His Church, and to His kingdom. This is importance indeed! ". . . . anyone who attaches himself to the Lord is one spirit with him" (I Cor. 6.17). He becomes our life, our hope, our joy and our destiny.

THE YOKE OF CHRIST

Were there any conditions to receiving all these benefits? Yes! He said that we must shoulder His yoke and learn from him. At the time of Christ oxen were used for ploughing and a heavy wooden yoke was tied to them for this purpose. So it seems that Jesus is offering to relieve us of burdens by replacing the existing ones with new ones! No prisoner ever asks for a new pair of handcuffs. The old ones are fine, thank you! The prisoner wants the chains removed.

What is Jesus saying? For one thing he is saying that

he understands human nature very well, for we insist on serving someone, either self, the world, Satan or God. But we will find a master to serve and a leader to follow, be they political, social or religious. The masters who hold our attention longest are the ones who demand our complete service, not less than everything. Hence false prophets and various "isms" always have their devoted adherents. Listen to Jesus in Matthew 6.24: "No one can be the slave of two masters: he will either hate the first and love the second, or be attached to the first and despise the second. You cannot be the slave both of God and of money."

It is a well-known axiom that nature abhors a vacuum, so Jesus understood that to remove us from the service of Satan and self he had to put us into the service of God. He had to remove the unbearable slavery of sin and Satan from us, and replace it with His own sweet yoke of commitment to God's will in everything. He could not leave us in a moral no-man's-land as the psychological society wants to do today, where one can choose one's own value systems without reference to anyone else, and in the absence of commitment. In this system "I want" reigns, which leads to chaos. When Jesus puts His yoke on us, God's "I want" for us, for our neighbours, and for the world reigns, and this leads to order, community and social progress.

The kingdoms of this world must give way to the kingdom of our Lord and of His Christ where the One who loves us all is the Master and Lord; where the one law in that kingdom is the Law of Love (John 13.34). It is this command to love that is the gentle yoke of Christ. He lived it himself first, and then challenged us to go out and conquer the world with it. Those who live by his royal law of love are on the road to heaven, in the right direction. If you want to check if you are on this road look at the actual people in your life, and ask yourself if you truly love and serve them. It is easy to talk of loving people in distant lands. Those who share the daily grind are another matter!

Jesus also said that we were to learn from him, for he was meek and humble of heart, and then we would find rest for our souls. Jesus is not only the Master, but the model we are to copy. He shows us how we are to live our lives in the world if we are to reach our destiny. We must study Him, both in the scriptures and in personal prayer and contemplation. The reason for this is that we are imitators, who copy their models, like the young people with their "pin-ups". We have to imitate Jesus' perfect obedience to the Father in everything, his love and reverence for everyone, his humility before his own creatures, and his untiring service to others no matter what the cost to himself.

Of all the virtues that he could choose from he picked out humility and meekness as two attitudes of soul that bring us rest. There is something about these two virtues that stills that knawing dissatisfaction inside of us that always wants more; that thing which says that everything we have experienced is nothing to what we should experience. Humility and meekness heal it! Yet of all possible virtues the world considers these two incomprehensible, and not worthy of adult, independent and self-governing lives. They smack of the "doormat" mentality that we shun even in others.

Let us look at them briefly. Humility is lowliness of heart. It is a sense of truth about oneself that neither exaggerates nor diminishes reality. Pride puffs us up in a ridiculous way, but humility sees, knows and accepts reality. We are what we are. Don't pretend to be either great or small. People's opinions don't alter the facts. If someone thinks we're great that does not make us great. If they think otherwise, that does not change anything. We remain free of both and keep our peace. There will always be people who are greater and lesser than ourselves; those who are more holy and more sinful, and people who are more important in the eyes of the world. What does it matter? We are what we are by the grace of God. We know our unimportance. There will be no crisis in the country when we die. Instead, it will be business as usual, for most of us do not have the power to stop the traffic. Does this stop us from serving? No, it frees us to serve! The humble and lowly ones are the happiest people on earth. It is the proud who are unhappy.

THE NARROW GATE

Jesus said, "Enter by the narrow gate, since the road that leads to destruction is wide and spacious, and many find it; but it is a narrow gate and a hard road that leads to life, and only a few find it" (Matt. 7.13–14). The invitation involves a lifetime of choices made with the help of grace. Grace is that divine help given to those who are open to receive it. It makes possible what is impossible to human nature by itself, but it is not passively received. One must actively seek it and use it. In so doing we cooperate with God's will and work in our lives. It is the divine enabling given to the generous person seeking God and life, and wanting to complete the journey desired by God.

The first choice is the road itself. We see the world go on its merry way as if life was meant to be "a good time" camp, where we enjoy ourselves, instead of a training ground for something greater. The attractiveness of the world's way does not require comment, only grace to resist the pull. It is difficult to swim against the tide of public opinion, to be "a loner", different from the crowd. "Oh, come on! everyone's doing it!" they say. It seems so crazy to deliberately choose the hard road, and to believe, let alone convince anyone else, that it is the better one. They think we are masochists wanting something that involves trials and difficulties, where one is expected to embrace sorrow and suffering.

Is it so crazy? Why then do explorers choose such a hard road for themselves? Why do they risk life and limb just to conquer a mountain, or find the North Pole? Why do astronauts risk everything to go into space? Why do weathermen fly into hurricanes? Why do scientists walk on the sea bed and carry out dangerous experiments? Why do human beings take risks that involve their very lives? Why? Because if we listen to our innermost beings we were made to be conquerors! And we are only happy when we are fighting every inch of the way.

No one is happy when life is handed to them on a plate, so to speak. We do not appreciate things given to us for nothing. Life must have a purpose, something to reach out for, something to risk life and limb for. There must be something out there to fight for, otherwise we die of boredom and meaninglessness. That is why we love entertainment that involves adventure and risk. And lives must be lost and won too, for that is the drama we joined as we stepped on to the stage of life.

Yes, Jesus understood us, and he gave us a hard road to conquer both for ourselves and for him, so that we could say with St Paul that we had finished the race and reached out for the prize of eternal life awaiting those who completed the journey (Phil. 3.9–16). Paul was not content just to make the trip. He turned it into a race for the finish. He wasted no time in this precious journey for he wanted his Master to be proud of him at the end: "I have fought the good fight to the end; I have run the race to the finish; I have kept the faith; all there is to come for me now is the crown of uprightness which the Lord, the upright judge, will give me on that Day . . ." (2 Tim. 4.6–8).

Observe the dedication of those who conquered Mount Everest, the lengthy preparations, the study of the mountain and the conditions of the climb. No one would attempt the climb unprepared, for it would be suicidal. The climbers needed vision, grit and determination as well as scientific knowledge. The right food, clothes and equipment would not suffice in sub-zero temperatures in a battle against the forces of nature. They needed the right motivation and the companionship of others on the way. Two would succeed where one would fail, for the sheer fear evoked by the forces of nature would be too great for a lone climber. Note, too, how many began the climb and the number that finished it. Two completed the climb, the two who refused to give up even when it seemed crazy to go on, but they went on to conquer the mountain – and to world fame.

The spiritual life is like that. Romans 15.4 says, "For everything that was written in the past was written to teach us, so that through endurance and the encouragement of the scriptures we might have hope" (NIV). The number who began the journey can be counted in millions, but the number who finish is small, because like the other mountain climbers they give up somewhere along the way for various reasons. We want to consider some of these reasons here.

SELF KNOWLEDGE, THE KEY

Just as mountain climbers need to study the climb, so do we. Preparation is vital if success is to follow. Like the climb, this journey may seem glamorous before the event, but we may not relish the bitter cold, the silence, the loneliness, the daily grind that rob the trip of its glamour. We may not have cleared our motivation, so that when things get tough we lack perseverance. If we are to climb the mountain of the Lord we need more grit and determination than any climber, for it is not just our physical life that is at stake, but our eternal life. To want an easy life in these circumstances is preposterous. This journey is not for fairweather Christians! It is for the valiant soldiers of Christ who will go forth to conquer themselves first for Christ, and then go out to conquer the world for him. For "the kingdom of heaven has been subjected to violence and the valiant are taking it by force" (Matt. 11.12).

There are choices to be made at every step of this journey, for the road narrows all the way until there is only room for one on the final stage of this exciting but dangerous trip. At this point we must choose God to the loss of everything! Then we are free at last, free to fly . . . but we are ahead of ourselves here! The clearer we make the choices the quicker the journey.

Ignorance of self is the greatest hindrance to this journey. Without self-knowledge we cannot grow in holiness because we cannot make the first step, which is to face our *real sinfulness* as distinct from admitting that we are all flawed and in need of some kind of help – although some won't even admit this much! If we refuse to acknowledge our real sins, then we prevent ourselves from experiencing Jesus as *our real Saviour*. This leaves us trapped in the tunnels of our own subconscious, at the mercy of all the psychological tricks that humans get up to to hide from themselves their true condition.

A refusal to admit sinfulness blinds us spiritually (see Isa. 44.20). It enables us to develop a false sense of self-confidence (Rev. 3.17) while retaining sin in the heart (John 9.41). It leads to ignorance of God's will (Mic. 4.12), and then it can even lead us to resist God and to oppose Him (John 15.21; 16.3). Thus we cannot take the journey at all. We become onlookers, armchair Christians, who know it all in theory while experiencing nothing. We are hearers of the Word, but not doers, and so we draw condemnation upon ourselves (Jas. 1.22–27). Jesus might have to say the same to us as he said to Philip one day: "Have I been with you all this time, Philip, and you still do not know me?" (John 14.9).

The opposite of this is in a little rhyme my father taught us as children

> Friend, learn to know yourself,
> and for this knowledge labour,
> change those things within yourself,
> that you condemn so in your neighbour.

If we are to journey successfully, then it is imperative that we learn first to know God, then to know ourselves. Then we learn to forget ourselves in loving God! It's very simple. It just requires a lot of grace and perseverance, but the rewards are great even in the here-and-now of time. The saints tell us that to love God we must change much, so a commitment to self-knowledge is not just self-analysis such as the psychologists are interested in. No. It is useful knowledge, living knowledge, which prepares for grace and redemption. If there is generosity in the soul, then the Lord will give an abundance of self-knowledge to hasten progress on the journey. This stage will be short or long depending on our willingness to learn and to change with grace.

This self-knowledge is acquired from observing one's own actions, from listening to others reflect on our behaviour, by meditating on the Word of God, and by seeking spiritual counsel from someone ahead of us who will be objective, sympathetic and loving in their approach: Listen to Ecclesiasticus 37.7–15: "Any adviser will offer advice, but some are governed by self-interest. Beware of someone who offers advice; first find out what he wants himself – since his advice coincides with his own interest – in case he has designs on you. . . . But have constant recourse to some devout person, whom you know to be a keeper of the commandments, whose soul matches your own, and who, if you go wrong, will be sympathetic. Finally, stick to the advice that your own heart gives you, no one can be truer to you than that; since a person's soul often gives a clearer warning than seven watchmen perched on a watchtower. And besides all this beg the Most High to guide your steps into the truth."

The whole journey is a proces of becoming, or being born again into the new life of the resurrection, so it is imperative that everything in the flesh life be put under the power and influence of grace. Or to use St Paul's language, the old man must die in us so that the new man can emerge: "You must give up your old way of life; you must put aside your old self, which gets corrupted by following illusory desires. Your mind must be renewed by a spiritual revolution so that you can put on the new self that has been created in God's way, in the goodness and holiness of the truth" (Eph. 4.22–24).

This will involve us in many battles with ourselves that would match the forces of nature in ferocity any day! It is one thing to tackle external things. It takes greater courage, guts, to tackle the enemy within, and the stakes are higher too. Moral courage is needed, and grim determination not to give up, for you will praise God all your life for the victories won at this stage. They are vital for all the other stages. Just as one cannot skip a stage on the mountain climb, so one cannot skip a stage here. Each step must be taken with great care, and no hard-won victory must be lost or discouragement will set in and this is deadly for perseverance.

WHAT SELF-KNOWLEDGE DO WE NEED?

If we are beginning the journey then we need to know that adults have what is called a public self, a private self, a hidden self and an unconscious self, and you thought you were simple!

Who am I?

public self private self	hidden self unconscious self

What part of this do I operate out of? Am I in control of my own self?

The public self is that part of us that we project to others, our professional image; what we want others to see. Unless we want to be hypocrites this must be the true image reflecting what is on the inside of us. The private self is what we know of ourselves but do not want others to know. This is the dark side which must come under the rod of repentance so that we become integrated, whole persons.

The hidden self is a real problem, for it is that part of us that others see, but which we may refuse to look at. Those who live with us know this part of us well, and can help with information if we are humble enough to take it, for it shows up in our behaviour and they suffer from it. This too, must go under the rod of repentance even if we are to love the very people we say that we love. The most difficult area of all is the unconscious self, the hidden motivations that are not only hidden from others, but also from ourselves. Have you ever wondered why you do certain things? Yet these hidden motivations influence our lives powerfully for good or ill. Here we need to come before the Lord in prayer and ask for enlightenment. Often we need the help of a spiritual director to come to grips with this area too.

SOME AREAS THAT NEED TO BE DEALT WITH

Let us call the following areas "road blocks" which make the journey impossible. Therefore they must be dealt with. The whole idea is that we want to get on with the journey quickly, so removing obstacles forms part of the preparation for the climb.

The Area of Personal Habits: We are creatures of habit, and may not consider that some of our habitual responses to life may be lethal to the spiritual journey.

Here we have basic attitudes like selfishness, laziness or carelessness concerning one's obligations in life. Also attitudes towards others like snobbishness, fault finding, pride and arrogance, etc. (see Matt. 23.1–7).

Personal Sin: which we are finding difficulty dealing with. If there is *deliberate sin* in our lives, no matter how small, it is an effective block, one that prevents growth, happiness, healing and wholeness. It is not possible to have permanent peace as long as sin reigns in our mortal bodies – to use St Paul's words again. Those who attempt the climb without eradicating deliberate sin are destined to live at the foot of the mountain, not because grace is ineffective, but because it has not been used.

Past Hurts: When past hurts have not been dealt with they give rise to a host of problems in the area of resentments, bitterness and self-pity. They can also contribute to a sense of failure and low self-worth. These things are too dangerous to take with us. They must be handled by forgiveness and inner healing.

Self-Will: You are bent on doing something regardless of consequences, or any consideration. Some people are so stubborn in their own opinion that they are quietly immovable. Everyone else must adapt to them, but there is no question of changing for the sake of anyone else. They refuse to listen to others, so they do not know what listening to God is. This is highly dangerous for those who need to journey with the Lord, for there is constant change and adaptation required all along the way.

Human Respect: This is also called the "fear of man",

and it means that a person is governed by public opinion instead of principle, afraid to act on conviction because of what others think. They won't risk criticism, so they "play to the gallery" in life. No possibility of a climb here, for we must act according to God's will in everything, even if everyone is against us.

Manipulation of Others: Anyone who manipulates or controls others is not free enough to undertake the arduous journey. They need to be freed to become persons in their own right, motivated by higher principles, free to act according to God's will before they commence the climb. Manipulation and control of others is the way the world governs its affairs, but is alien to the kingdom of God where each person is reverenced and respected in their own right.

Criticism and Gossip: One of the hardest areas to control is the tongue, but it must be put under the discipline of God's will, for we do more damage with the tongue than with anything else. The Book of Proverbs has 50 proverbs on the tongue alone so this is not a new problem. Here are two of them: "Deep waters, such are human words: a gushing stream, the utterance of wisdom". "Death and life are in the gift of the tongue, those who indulge it must eat the fruit it yields" (Prov. 18.4; 21). If we are to harness our energies for the journey then we cannot afford the dissipation of the negative use of the tongue. The tongue will be needed to give life, and healing, and to proclaim the gospel. How can the Holy Spirit be expected to anoint a dirty tongue? Or one that destroys reputations? Or one that refuses to forgive?

Many other areas could be mentioned, but let us

finish by reminding ourselves that an inability to face reality *today* means that no journey will be undertaken. If we are sincere in seeking God, then He will show us what are the specific blocks in our own make-up that hinder the journey. When these are removed, off we go!

WHY DO SOME PEOPLE NOT GROW?

Why did most of the climbers on Everest not make it to the top of the mountain? Some stopped at stage one, others at stage two. Why? Why do the vast majority of Christians not become saints (in the accepted sense)? Why do statistics show that a large majority of adults do not mature fully? When you look at them you observe stunted growth. Let us look at some of the reasons in the hope that this will free more of us to get up and go on, when times get tough.

The first reason is fear, one of the most crippling emotions known. What are we afraid of? The common fears are fear of the unknown, fear of the future, fear of death, fear of failure, fear of letting go and fear of insecurity. They can be all summed up in the fear of change. Growth is full of the unexplored, and therefore demands constant change. Observe the Simon Peter of the gospels and the Christian leader of the Acts and you see someone who has changed almost out of recognition. For Peter became a monument to the grace of God, and a glory to Jesus, and His power to save. Peter is a good advertisement for the gospel he preached. His message could have been summed up as follows: "If he did this to me, he can do it for you!"

Paul, too, is another example of the transforming power of grace, for here the Lord changed a closed, bigoted, self-righteous Pharisee into a pure firebrand for God. The transformation of Saul into Paul was dramatic, shocking and wonderful. Peter and Paul, two rivals in the race to the finish, show what a wonderful effect it has on the world if someone would only persevere to the end. These men dramatically changed the course of human history. Their struggle turned out to be vital for the whole human race, just as the astronaut who walked on the moon did it for us all. Through him we all walked on the moon, and we all climbed Mount Everest in those brave men who conquered it. They were small steps for the men, but giant leaps for mankind.

In the same way Jesus wants us to die and rise through his death and resurrection, so that the whole human race can walk in newness of Life. How thrilling! Our private struggles on this journey are, in fact, vital for the human race. It makes us very important actors on the stage of human history.

Many people use fear as an excuse not to grow. Growth is uncomfortable and unsettling and cuts across our tendency *to settle down*, a tendency that grows with the years. We like to take the easy way out of things, one that does not involve growth. Yet if we settle down too quickly, or too well, we fossilize, and this is not the type of monument the Lord wants! We must examine our refusals to grow, for they are enlightening. When confronted by some new truth about ourselves many say: "But I've always been this way!" "This is me; this is what I'm like!" But this is precisely what those who love us want us to change in order to make us *more* lovable. To stay the way we always were is to refuse to change and grow, to remain stunted as a person. Those who love us put up with it and suffer. If we are like this in ordinary everyday life, do you think that we are any different in prayer? Would we be open to a challenge from the Lord? The bad news is that we are the same person in prayer and out of it. If we are closed, we're closed.

A refusal to grow is also a refusal to use our talent, and to play our part on the world stage. In the parable of the talents (Matt. 15.14–30) Jesus compared himself to a king going away to a far country (Heaven), leaving his kingdom in the hands of his servants (the Church, us). Each one was gifted according to his ability, so some had more gifts than others, some less. After a long time (the Church age) the master returned (in the Second Coming), and each one had to give an account of his use of his gifts. There was judgment for those who refused to play their part in the work given them. Burying the talent and leaving it unused was unacceptable to the Master, who was not interested in excuses, or theories about religion that made God out to be unjust (v. 24).

The parable finishes with this "good-for-nothing servant" thrown out into the darkness (God is light) where there will be weeping and gnashing of teeth (Hell is the total frustration of the person destined for the glory of God). This good-for-nothing servant refused the challenge to grow and develop, so the master took his talent from him and gave it to the person who had been the most generous in responding to life. Grace abounded for this person, whereas judgment met the one who refused to live and grow. Put yourself in God's place and ask yourself how you would feel if one of your creatures refused the opportunities you gave them to become someone great. This servant is a "has-been", an "also-ran", someone whose glory and achievements are all in their yesterdays. They are easily forgotten. But we don't easily forget Peter and Paul!

People who have stopped growing easily bore us, for their life and behaviour are predictable. There is no mystery to them. We quickly realize that we know all there is to them, while they settle down to a false self-acceptance that makes them smug. This enables them to criticize others, especially those who are still growing, for these continue to make mistakes, and suffer the insecurity of learning new things, and of walking by faith into an unpredictable future, but one full of hope. The others have insured themselves against all eventualities, and settle down to a comfortable, if boring, existence. But it is not Christian! And it is not life. A ship in a harbour is safe, but that is not what ships were made for! An aircraft on the ground may be safe, but it is also ridiculous, for it was made to soar into the heavens, and ride on the wings of the wind, just as the ship was made to ride the oceans and battle the storms. If they refuse to do this, where is the justification for their existence? They become museum pieces, nostalgic reminders of the past.

Is an adult who has stopped growing attractive? Do they have anything that would draw another to them? Think of an infant, utterly helpless, totally dependent on its parents for everything, yet amazingly attractive. Everyone loves babies because they symbolize new life. They have all the mystery and mystique of an actively growing person. Everyone wants to know what will they become? We watch every move, and teach the child as much as possible. We delight in their victories, no matter how small. They are the centre of attention, and we never lose interest because they are in a process of becoming. But suppose you visited that house twenty years later and found the "baby" still in nappies and sucking from a bottle, would you be happy? If they had stopped growing at six months and fossilized in that position would you rejoice? No! We would break our hearts at a tragedy that robbed this person of the fullness of life. Were they brought into existence to suck all their lives? Oh no! What would bring us joy would be a full grown twenty year old, full of life and entering into the fullness of adulthood. In the same way Jesus declared that he came on earth for a reason: "I have come so that they may have life and have it to the full" (John 10.10). It is no joy to the Lord to look upon his people half-redeemed, with stunted spiritual growth, having no power to transform the world. He did not die to leave us like this!

THE CHALLENGE TO GROW

There is a lovely passage in Matthew 14.22–33 that shows us a growing point for Peter. After the miracle of the loaves, Jesus sent his Apostles out onto the Lake of Galilee to get away from the pressure of the crowds. After making their escape Jesus himself dismissed the crowds he had fed so marvellously. Then he took the opportunity of some time alone with the Father in solitude and prayer. Meanwhile the Apostles were having a difficult time on the lake with high winds and heavy seas. Jesus left them to deal with the situation all night, then he came to their rescue walking on the very waters that they could hardly handle! What a shock for them! In the dim light just before dawn, they thought that they were seeing things and cried out in fear. Jesus called to them not to be afraid, that it was only himself!

This was the challenge. Jesus was walking on the

water that threatened their lives. Peter and the others were confronted with a new reality. How would they react? Peter decided to test the situation: "Lord", he said "if it is you, tell me to come to you across the water." Jesus said, "Come" (v. 28). At this, Peter stepped out into the unknown to try something he had never even considered possible before. Don't be surprised that he failed on the first attempt! We are not experts the first time we do anything. We learn by our mistakes. Nevertheless, as he stepped out of that boat the Christian standard rose so high that I wonder if it has been surpassed. Looking firmly into the eyes of Jesus, Peter knew that everything is possible to those who believe (see Mark 9.23). He stepped out of the boat on to the turbulent sea.

What about the other eleven in the boat? They were in the same circumstances, with the very same Jesus! Would they risk failure? or the insecurity of the new thing? It is a frightening thing to grow, but also exhilarating. Fear keeps us stunted and wizened like plants afraid of the wind and the rain. Not one of them followed Peter out into the unknown. They understood boats, not walking on water. Refusing the risk, they chose the security of the known and the predictable, and lost a golden opportunity to grow. Oh, but did they secretly hope that Peter would make a fool of himself? If he did, then they could criticize his foolishness and lecture him on prudence, as this would make them feel more secure in their refusal.

Peter went down all right, when he took his eyes off Jesus to look at the staggering feat he had accomplished by simple faith alone. Once his attention went on to self-reflection, he lost the vision that would take him the rest of the way. So he merited the gentle loving rebuke of his Master: "Why did you doubt?" Then with Jesus at his side Peter returned to the boat walking on the water alongside his beloved Master. What was impossible to him by himself was possible with Jesus. The standard is still too high for the fainthearted!

TOO WEAK

One of the favourite excuses for not growing is that we claim to be too weak. Many people give the impression that we must have dealt with all sin and weakness before undertaking the climb. This is untrue, for the trip is the journey of salvation. The Peter who walked on the water was not a perfected person. No. He had a long way to go, and there were pitfalls ahead for him. We don't grow in spite of our faults, but because of them! It is in facing our faults, repenting and allowing the Lord to teach us His ways, that we grow. We actually grow through our faults. Jesus knows that "the spirit is willing but the flesh is weak" (Matt. 26.41), so we must struggle with temptations, passions and desires to obey God's will.

Often it is the moment of greatest sinfulness, or failure, that is the turning point of our lives. It was so for Peter. Simon Bar Jona became Peter the Rock on the night he discovered that with a *little pressure* he denied Jesus in dreadful circumstances. To save his own skin he denied that he ever knew Him. This is a far cry from walking on water! This night he learned the opposite of that other night. It was his faith and trust in Jesus that made walking on water possible. Now trust in himself and in human nature unaided by grace meant that nothing was possible, not even fidelity to the Master he loved so much. What a lesson! However,

Peter learned that lesson, and cried his way to repentance and freedom. He was manly enough to admit he had done wrong, and *to change.*

Judas also denied Jesus that night, but refused to learn, or to repent, so he shrivelled up in fear and died. Peter accepted his mistake, and Jesus' forgiveness, and lived to become a good shepherd to other sinners who needed to find eternal life. Peter grew through that experience of sin and forgiveness, for he was open to learn and to live. He did not refuse the self-knowledge needed for growth. He was not too proud to learn, hence he remained a beloved apostle of Jesus, and ended his career by giving his life for the very One he had denied! (Proverbs 3.1–12).

DISCOURAGEMENT

Anyone who ever attempted Everest knows what discouragement is. From a distance the mountain is awesome as it rises in beauty, the joy of all the earth. But if you are still at the stage of writing lyric poetry about it, you've never attempted the climb! Just so the Mountain of the Lord inspires awe and wonder even in unbelievers, who admire the climbers but without joining them. As we stand at the foot of the Hill of Calvary and look at the path ahead, it has an austere beauty, a splendour in its outline, with the Tree of the Cross (the tree of Life) at its summit. Valley-dwelling Christians may speak with enthusiasm of their faith. From this point of view it is easy to talk of the incomparable loveliness of the Christian ideal. They feel a poetic ecstasy as they contemplate the Everlasting Hills from the comfort of their own armchairs, just as football fans rave about their team even though they may never know the discomfort of football in the mud and rain, or what it is to sustain serious injury from the game.

For the more serious Christian, the silent, dogged, climber of the mountain, the pilgrim on the Way of the Cross, there is little opportunity for aesthetic admiration of the beautiful landscape. They may not even notice it, because all their energies are taken up with the climb itself, and with sheer survival! The climber *has become part of the glorious picture* admired by others less adventuresome. They have accepted its life, and therefore cannot see it any more, save for those rare moments of vision. What they do see is the next bit of loose gravel or stony path which must be trodden, the difficult rocks which cannot be avoided, the unending slope which gets steeper; the growing weakness, the solitude, the burden, and the cumulative hardships and burdens on the way.

It is not difficult to see that the problem here is discouragement. Once we overcome the fear of growing we lose heart very quickly when we seem to get no results from our efforts at correcting our faults. We are tempted to give up, to stop trying and then to take refuge in cynicism or bitterness. We want to pretend that it was all a dream. "It was only fizz", they say. "It wasn't real". "It's all over now, and I have to get back to normal" . . . whatever that is. Hopefully it does not mean going back to sin, unbelief and worldliness, for that is tragedy. This is where perseverance and the will to endure carry the day. We have to learn from the hard knocks of life not to become hard, but to become supple and resilient. Most people give up too soon . . . sometimes a few yards from victory.

We are so like those two men on the Road to

Emmaus (Luke 24.13–35). They were thoroughly discouraged by the events of Holy Week. "We had hoped . . ." they said, but now they were leaving Jerusalem just as the news of victory was about to break! They had believed Jesus was the Messiah, but now things were bleak. The women told them Jesus was risen from the dead, but instead of rejoicing, or even checking the facts, they considered this the last straw! They turned around and left Jerusalem. It didn't really matter where they were going. Jesus had to join them, and gently lead them back to Jerusalem and the destiny that God had waiting for them there. He did this through a study of the holy scriptures, and talking with them in prayer. Then as their hearts began to open to Him and to truth once again, they invited him into their home and he revealed Himself fully in the Holy Eucharist. Then he sent them back on the right road in the right direction, armed with the scriptures, with personal prayer and the Eucharist, the three breads for the journey, without which we have no hope of arriving at our destination.

Lovely poetry and music are no use to the climber. They must be fed from within if they are to survive, for the journey is taken in a world full of sinfulness, conflict, corruption and disease. The inner vision must be fed to keep eyes fixed on the goal. Besides, we are not alone. Jesus, who made the journey from heaven to earth in the incarnation, and who made the return journey successfully in his passion and resurrection, now *joins us on our journey into life*. He is at our side, and within our hearts, teaching, guiding, enlightening and strengthening all the way. We do not attain our end by contemplating the glory from a distance, but by the blood and guts of the pilgrim way.

Jesus walks with us helping us to carry our cross, not

the glorious cross that we sing about, but our own rough, clumsy, home-made copy which the pilgrim must carry all the way. We have his promises to keep us going too: "Do not let your hearts be troubled. You trust in God, trust also in me . . . I am going now to prepare a place for you . . . I shall return to take you to myself, so that you may be with me where I am. You know the way to the place where I am going . . . I am the way; I am the truth, and the life" (John 14.1–16).

There is a strange awesomeness about the pilgrims and their invisible companion going, as Moses did, to meet God on the mountain. This strange harsh road, so insulting to our "joy-philosophy" generation, remains the only path to wisdom and love. The radiant Moses who descended the Mountain of God armed with God's revelation for the whole world had been the weary climber a little while before (Exodus 19–34). We forget that the supreme moment of meeting God on the mountain had been preceded by the stern and lonely struggle upwards in dust, heat and breathlessness, that possessed few moments of dignity and romance.

Patience is the cure for discouragement. The willingness to endure setbacks, failures and frustrations for the sake of the Lord. This is the power that transforms the signs of death into the sources of life, grace, strength, and above all, HOPE. Fortitude (steel for your soul) is needed too. The higher the skyscraper, the deeper into the earth must go the foundations. The pilgrim must not fear going down into the depths of their own darkness and discouragement. Just invite Jesus and the Holy Spirit to join you there, to enlighten the darkness, then you emerge on the resurrection side, victorious and free.

Psalm 23.4 says: "Even were I to walk in a ravine as

dark as death I should fear no danger, for you are at my side . . .". Psalm 139.7–12 instructs us similarly: "Where shall I go to escape your spirit? Where shall I flee from your presence? . . . I will say: 'Let the darkness cover me, and the night wrap itself around me' but even darkness to you is not dark, and night is as clear as the day". When discouragement hits us, let us imitate the desert plants. Let us push our roots deep into the soil until they reach the bedrock (Christ), and only then unfold our leaves to the sun (God's love) so we will not be destroyed by the sandstorms.

POSSESSIVENESS

The last obstacle to taking the journey that we want to consider just now is the problem of possessiveness. Growth is only possible where there is liberty of spirit, where one is free enough to travel. Let us compare the rich young man of Luke 18.18–23 and Zacchaeus, the rich man of Luke 19.1–10. Both were rich, but did the money possess them or did they possess the money? Jesus loved them both, and offered new life to both of them regardless of the fact that the young man got his wealth by inheritance and Zacchaeus got his by dubious means. One was money from a right source and the other was from a wrong source.

When challenged by Jesus the young man refused to risk the new life, for he was attached to his money and all the privileges that it secured. He couldn't leave all to find all and he went away sad. Zacchaeus, on the other hand, without any words from Jesus, was so moved by the fact that Jesus would pay attention to the likes of him, that he immediately offered to give half of his fortune to the poor, and to pay back fourfold anyone he had cheated, something not demanded by the law at all! Here we have the usual Lukan quandary: the "goodie" is bad and the "baddie" is good! ("Good" here refers to openness to new life, openness to grace and salvation, not to any quantity of moral uprightness).

The difference between the two men was an interior attitude to life. The young man was possessive whereas the older one was not. Zacchaeus knew that it was wise to give up what he could not keep to gain what he could not lose. This wisdom was lost on the younger man. Possessiveness destroys freedom. It robs us of the ability to give and receive, and both are necessary for growth. Christianity stands for unpossessiveness, that is, poverty and dependance on God for everything. So many people tie themselves down to a way of life that demands certain possessions. They take jobs they dislike in order to obtain the possessions they think they should have, thereby joining a treadmill that causes unhappiness, and a sense of futility. "Martha, Martha, you worry and fret about so many things, and yet few are needed, indeed only one. It is Mary who has chosen the better part . . ." (Luke 10.41–42).

Material possessions are not the only problem here, for many people are possessive about relationships. They take people over and claim them as their own property. No one else may share the friendship. Some husbands put their wives under house arrest because of their possessiveness, refusing to allow them to have any friends of their own. Some people are possessive about themselves, refusing to share themselves with others, refusing their time, talents, maybe even their smile. It's an effective way to avoid challenge.

The law of the Spirit of Life in Christ Jesus demands that we open up to life, to giving, to growth. The more we give of ourselves the more we can receive. We can only grow if we let go of whatever it is we are holding on to, be they material things, persons, ideas, opinions, whatever. We must hold life lightly, always willing to let go of yesterday's bread in order to receive today's bread today from the Lord. If we are to be open to today's experiences, we must let our yesterdays go, for the more we hold on to what was, the more we prevent what is and what is to become.

Real freedom is the ability to give from the heart and of the heart. Unless we do this we give nothing. Freedom to be ourselves also implies a certain independence with regard to the multitude of influences that seek to form us. We must continuously sift out the good from the bad, and thus grow in discernment of God's specific will for us personally (I Thess. 5.21). Finally, to grow we must live in the present, in the here-and-now, with reality as it presents itself to us. Part of that reality is that we are limited in our choices by a whole range of external and internal factors at any given time. There is also the fact that we have so many defence mechanisms that prevent us seeing objective reality, and from opening up fully to God and to life. But if we know this we will understand our need for daily prayer and enlightenment.

MR SHIP/HER LADYSHIP

Let us conclude with a story, one that illustrates the seriousness of the decision to begin the journey NOW. This is a parable about a young family on holiday. Here is the key so that we can interpret it as we go along. The father is God, the mother is Mary, and the boy is Jesus. Mr Ship or Her Ladyship is you and me.

The boy is about twelve years of age, so the family decide to go to a country place by the sea because the son loves adventure. On the very first day the boy found a hidden cove protected by the cliffs along the hinterland. He was so excited that he dashed back to the camp to tell his parents all about it. It was a sailing ship that he found, but it was up on the sand almost hidden from view by the protective cliffs. He was intrigued, for what was a ship doing there? Ships were made to plough the oceans and battle the winds and the waves. What was it doing there all hidden from life? Perhaps it had been shipwrecked, he would go and investigate. That first evening the parents got a full description of the ship, and they knew that the adventure had begun.

Dawn the following day saw the boy, breakfasted, going towards the cliffs, and the day's events. First, he had to find a safe way down those steep cliffs, for this was but the beginning of what was to become daily visits. (Clue: the shepherd goes looking for the lost sheep: grace precedes salvation.) The ship was examined very carefully that day. The boy needed signs of damage. He must assess the situation before enlisting his dad's help. He also tried to get a reaction from the ship, but failed that day. No matter, he would try again tomorrow (This may be your first talking ship!)

The following day the same ritual occurred, except that the boy began to instruct Mr Ship on why ships were made. He talked about wonderful adventures at sea. The ocean was a symbol of life's journey. There were two shores, the earthly one where the journey began, and the heavenly one where the journey finished. The quantity of water in the ocean represented the all-sufficiency of grace to take you there. And then the wind, the glorious wind, represented the Holy Spirit, the One who guided the journey from start to finish. It was not necessary to be a wonderful ship, the greatest thing that ever hit the ocean. No, it was only necessary to want to take the journey, and to trust oneself to the wind and the waves, and all would be well. Oh sure! There would be storms, high winds sometimes and heavy seas, but that would not stop you when you had all necessary help to complete the journey.

Mr Ship listened to all this enthusiasm in silence. "After all", he said to himself, "it was a child who was talking, obviously an idealistic child, who dreamed of great things. He must never have witnessed a storm at sea! He must never have experienced the terror of hurricanes, or twenty-foot waves crashing in on oneself. He was too young to know the dangers, that's why he was talking like that". He must have patience, for the child would surely give up and go away soon. "Childish enthusiasm doesn't last", he told himself. Then he settled back in his rut and slept, as far away from the wind and the waves as he could reasonably get without looking ridiculous.

But the child did not give up. He persevered each day visiting the ship, offering new life and hope, but all he got in response was that Mr Ship creaked and groaned from side to side and then settled back into his rut. Finally, one day Mr Ship lost patience with the boy's perseverance. He shouted back: "Go away! Yourself and your new ideas. What do you know about life? What do you know about the ocean and its terrors? Did your mother not even tell you about pirates on the seas? Go home and ask her about storms, and the number of ships that never made it to the other side! They lie right now at the bottom of the sea, forgotten by all. Go away and leave me alone. I have done what I can to make my miserable life as comfortable as possible. It isn't much, but it's the best that I can do. No wind will ever send me to the bottom of the ocean, for I'm staying right here."

The boy was very distressed with this response to all his loving care and attention, and went home to discuss the matter with his father. The father looked sadly at his son and said: "Son, don't break your heart over that old ship. He has been like that for so long that he may not WANT the new life that you are offering." The boy could not believe that, for surely everyone wanted life in all its fullness? Surely no one would refuse to take the journey? Could they possibly WANT to rot and fossilize where they were, and never know the reason why they were made? No, it's not possible! He just needed to try again. He mustn't have put the invitation properly.

So, in spite of all the rejections, the boy persevered day after day. He began to instruct the ship on how to leave its rut and sail again. He explained how the winds worked, and the tides and everything necessary for the launch, but with no response from Mr Ship that he could discern. Finally the boy went back to his dad to make a big request. "For my sake", he said, "would you give us a big wind and a big wave to help Mr Ship to get going? He needs a lot of help." His father agreed to the request on a given day when the boy had fully instructed Mr Ship.

Finally, the big day came that the boy had prepared the ship so carefully for. He was so excited because he could not accept that the ship would refuse all help. The wind was howling in the heavens and the seas were high and rough, just right for the re-launch of Mr Ship. The boy instructed the ship to move on the first turning of the tide, and then waited excitedly for the big moment. But the ship did not move, though it creaked and groaned more fiercely than ever before, for the wind dislodged it from its safe place and it rocked perilously about. The boy urged it to go now . . . now! But it refused to go. The moment of grace had passed.

As the tide moved out and the wind died down so the boy turned to the ship which he loved, and pronounced sentence on it: "You will never go anywhere now! You are only fit for the fire!" With that (for you know who the boy is) a terrible sound of breaking was heard, and the once great ship fell in a heap of ruins at the boy's feet. FIREWOOD. But the boy threw himself down in the sand and wept his heart out. He cried so much that he did not hear his father approaching. His father lifted him up and said; "My son, I told you not to break your heart over that old ship. He had made his decision. He did not WANT life. And not even God can save a soul that does not want to be saved! We gave him free will, and the right to choose. He has chosen death. So be it."

Postscript: It is no small matter to consider the Two Ways. Each of us is free to choose, but we must live out the consequences of our decision. It is a life and death matter which way we go. CHOOSE LIFE THEN!

Acknowledgment: The original idea for that story came from an American preacher whose name I have forgotten. The story as told is my own.